TADPOLE to FROG

Camilla de la Bédoyère

Quarto is the authority on a wide range of topics.

Quarto educates, entertains and enriches the lives of our readers—enthusiasts and lovers of hands-on living.

www.quartoknows.com

Words in **bold** are explained in the glossary on page 22.

First published in 2019 by QED Publishing,
an imprint of The Quarto Group.
The Old Brewery, 6 Blundell Street,
London N7 9BH, United Kingdom.
T (0)20 7700 6700 F (0)20 7700 8066
www.QuartoKnows.com

A catalogue record for this book is available from the British Library.

ISBN 978-1-78603-623-0

Manufactured in Shenzhen, China HH092018

9 8 7 6 5 4 3 2 1

MIX
Paper from responsible sources
FSC® C017606
www.fsc.org

Picture credits
(t=top, b=bottom, l=left, r=right, c=center, fc=front cover, bc=back cover)

Alamy
21tc Chris Hill / Alamy Stock Photo

Corbis
6t, bcr Martin B Withers/Frank Lane Picture Agency

FLPA
10–11 Wil Meinderts/FN/Minden, 20t Roger Tidman

Getty Images
18–19 Frank Greenaway, 20–21 Christoph Burki

naturepl.com
13 Jane Burton

NHPA
14r George Bernard, 15l George Bernard, 15r George Bernard,
16–17 Stephen Dalton, 17r T Kitchin & V Hurst

Photolibrary Group
1 Elliott Neep, 6–7 Elliott Neep

Shutterstock
fc Dirk Ercken, 2t Knorre, 3/12c Eric Isselee, 4l Dirk Ercken, 4-5 Eric Isselee, 5r John Arehart, bcl 7t Thomas Mounsey, 8-9 andrekoehn, 14-15 Steve Byland, 19br davemhuntphotography

CONTENTS

WHAT IS A FROG?

A frog is an **amphibian**. It spends part of its life living in water, and part of its life on land.

Toads and newts are also amphibians. Toads walk or crawl, but frogs jump.

A newt has a long, thin body and a tail.

Eye

Common frogs have smooth, damp skin and golden eyes.

Amphibians lay their eggs in water. They live in wet places, often near ponds or lakes.

Foot

Most toads have bumpy skin.

THE STORY OF A FROG

A young frog is called a **tadpole**. It looks different to an adult frog.

This small animal begins its life as an egg. The amazing story of how it becomes an adult frog is called its **life cycle**.

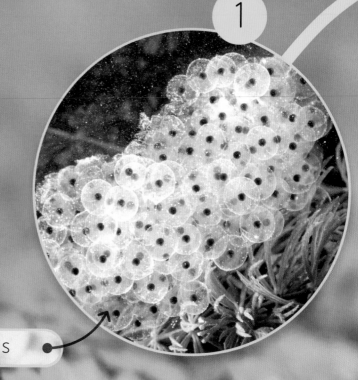

1

Eggs

2

Tadpole

A frog has three stages in its life cycle: egg, tadpole and adult.

3

Adult frog

FROGSPAWN

It is spring, and time for frogs to **mate**. Males croak loudly so the females can find them.

A male holds on to a female and she lays her eggs. He covers them with a liquid. It **fertilizes** the eggs. Only fertilized eggs grow into tadpoles.

The eggs are as soft as jelly. They stick together in a big clump called **frogspawn**.

The frogspawn swells and floats to the surface of the water.

INSIDE THE EGGS

The adult frogs swim away. They do not take care of the eggs.

Many of the eggs are eaten by fish and other pond animals. But some survive, and their tadpoles keep growing.

A female frog may lay hundreds of eggs at a time.

After a few weeks, the eggs hatch. They open up and a tadpole wriggles out of each one.

Inside each egg, a tadpole is growing. It feeds on a small yolk.

TINY TADPOLES

Tadpoles are tiny when they hatch, but they quickly grow.

Each tadpole has a long tail, which it uses to swim. It has feathery **gills** on either side of its head. A tadpole uses gills to breathe underwater.

To begin with, tadpoles just eat small, green water plants.

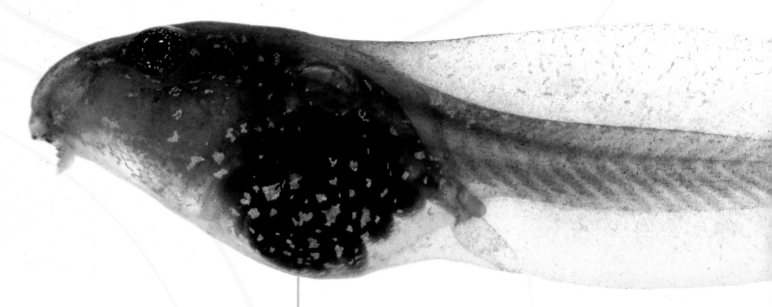

After a few weeks, the gills have disappeared. Now the tadpoles can eat pond animals, such as insects and water fleas.

Tadpoles eat and grow. They grow faster when they live in warm water with plenty of food.

Gills

Tail

THE BIG CHANGE

When they are about seven weeks old, tadpoles begin to change into frogs.

1

They grow four legs and their tails shrink. They swim to the surface of the pond to breathe air.

The tadpole's back legs grow first.

By the time it is 12 weeks old, the tiny frog is about 3 centimetres long.

2

Then its front legs begin to grow.

As its legs grow longer, the tail grows shorter.

3

The tadpoles now look like tiny frogs and they can leave the pond.

4

FROGLETS

The little frogs keep growing, and their tails disappear. They are now called froglets.

The froglets stay in, or near, water. They feed on small **insects**, which they catch with their long, sticky tongues.

Froglets can swim, crawl, hop and climb onto the floating leaves of lilies.

When they are bigger, the froglets move away from their pond.

They find a safe place under some plants, where they can hide.

This froglet is hiding in a pitcher plant in a wood.

17

THE LIFE OF A FROG

Adult frogs spend most of their time on land.

Frogs rest during the day. In the evening they hunt for insects, slugs and worms.

Many frogs have green, grey or brown skin. It is hard to see them when they sit still on plants, or under a pile of dead leaves. This is called **camouflage**.

Tongue

Frogs can make huge leaps to catch food with their long tongues.

Camouflage helps a frog to hide from animals that want to eat it.

BACK TO THE POND

Frogs **hibernate** in winter. This is because there is little food to eat, and the weather is cold.

When animals hibernate, they fall into a deep sleep to save energy.

Frogs hibernate under rocks, in burrows or in ponds.

In spring, frogs return to the pond where they hatched. This is where the adult frogs mate. Soon the story of the life cycle will begin again.

A male frog uses a bag of air in its throat to croak.

Frogs are ready to mate when they are two to three years old.

GLOSSARY

Amphibian
An animal that spends the first part of its life cycle in water, and the second part mostly on land.

Camouflage
Patterns and colours that help an animal to hide.

Fertilize
When liquid from a male changes female eggs so that they can grow into new living things.

Frogspawn
A clump of frog's eggs.

Gills
The parts of a tadpole's body that allow it to breathe underwater.

Hibernate
To spend the cold winter months in a kind of deep sleep.

Insect
A small animal with six legs. A water flea is a type of insect.

Life cycle
The story of how a living thing changes from birth to death and how it has young.

Mate
When a male and female animal come together to produce new life.

Tadpole
A very young frog that has hatched from an egg and lives all the time in water.

Yolk
The part of an egg that feeds the growing tadpole.

INDEX

NOTES FOR PARENTS AND TEACHERS

 Look through the book and talk about the pictures.

 Teach children how to stay safe while investigating animals and their life cycles, especially when they are around water.

 Teach children how to observe and, if appropriate, handle animals with care. They should observe animals in their natural environment, without disturbing wildlife and their habitats. Frogspawn should not be moved from one pond to another, as this allows viruses and other diseases to spread.

 Draw the life cycle of a frog and label the different stages together.

 Visit a wildlife garden or park together and learn about pond habitats. Talk about the ways that a habitat provides an animal with the food and shelter it needs to survive. Find out which other animals live in a pond habitat.

 Be prepared for questions about human life cycles. Talking about a child's family helps them to link life processes, such as reproduction, to their own experience. Drawing simple family trees and looking at photo albums are fun ways to engage young children.